Trail to the Klondike

by Don McCune

Washington State University Press
Pullman, Washington

Washington State University Press, PO Box 645910, Pullman, Washington 99164-5910
Phone: 800-354-7360, Fax: 509-335-8568
©1997 by the Board of Regents of Washington State University
All rights reserved
First printing 1997

The historic photographs used in this book were obtained by the late Don McCune from a variety of sources, including private collections. Many of these images are now in the collections of The University of Washington Libraries.

Library of Congress Cataloging-in-Publication Data

McCune, Don.
        Trail to the Klondike / Don McCune.
            p.   cm.
        Includes bibliographical references (p.   ).
        ISBN 0-87422-143-9 (cloth). — ISBN 0-87422-144-7 (pbk.)
        1. Alaska—History—1867-1969. 2. British Columbia—History. 3. Klondike River Valley (Yukon)—Gold discoveries. 4. Trails—Alaska—History—19th century. 5. Trails—British Columbia—History—19th century. 6. Alaska—History—1867-1969—Pictorial works.
7. British Columbia—History—Pictorial works.   I. Title.
F909.M49   1997
979.8'04—dc21   97-735
                                                                                            CIP

Acknowledgments

In selecting the Chilkoot Pass as part of a series dealing with the Klondike gold rush for *Exploration Northwest,* a weekly, true-life adventure program produced by KOMO TV in Seattle, Washington from 1960-1981, our objective was a "then-and-now" treatment which would combine the authenticity of the pictorial record with an on-the-spot description of the area as it is today. The "then" part had been taken care of earlier; the most notable contributor being E.A. Hegg, a Bellingham photographer who had supplied the world with its first glimpse of Klondike history in the making. The "now" part was up to us, the *Exploration Northwest* crew, consisting of: director Tim Bullard, cameramen Joel Schroedel and Bill Bacon, and myself. We were also accompanied by Gerry ter Haar, a free-lance photographer who joined us in Skagway, and Lyle Kleinschmidt, a fellow Klondike "buff" whose still-picture coverage has been used extensively throughout the book.

Original Klondike photos were obtained through the cooperation of Mr. Robert Monroe, director of the Special Collections Division, University of Washington Library. Special acknowledgment is given to Mrs. John Preston of Seattle, Washington for the use of a family diary, as well as to the memory of Ethel Anderson Becker, whose publications and photographic collection on the subject of the Klondike have long served as a personal source of inspiration. Special acknowledgment is also given to the Alaska-Yukon pioneers, whose friendship and encouragement motivated the project and, finally, to the many Klondikers whose stories will never be told yet whose struggle is evident through the eyes of the camera. It is to them that this book is respectfully dedicated.

Don McCune

Contents

Foreword

Had my husband, Don McCune, been born 100 years earlier, he would have been among those pioneers who headed west in wagons. He was an adventurer as a young man, and when he finished high school in 1937, he moved west from Illinois, hitchhiking with just a few dollars in his pocket, to eastern Washington, where he worked on his grandfather's farm.

In 1938 he joined the Civilian Conservation Corps and became a surveyor in Washington's Cascade mountains. He spent his days tramping through the woods to set surveying stakes, a job he loved.

Don was gifted with a sonorous voice and the ability to tell a good story. He became a Seattle radio disc jockey in 1943, and by 1949 he had an opportunity to become a radio station manager in Fairbanks, Alaska. Don felt right at home with the adventurous inhabitants of Alaska and soon created a radio show called *From Out of the North*. He researched and wrote about true adventures of the north country. It was then that he learned the story of the Klondike gold rush. Like the stampeders, Don, too, had headed to this country with hopes of finding his future. He was a stringer for NBC, recorded the official version of the *Alaska Flag Song,* and became known as "the voice of Alaska."

After ten years in Fairbanks, which included putting the town's first television station on the air and serving as general manager, KOMO Television lured Don back to Seattle. There he wrote and narrated a series called *Exploration Northwest,* a show that ran for twenty-one years, winning twenty-six Emmy Awards. These were adventures filmed throughout the greater Northwest and Don returned often to film stories in Alaska.

In 1964 he wrote and told the story of the Klondike gold rush. Knowing he could touch only the surface of the story in a half-hour show, he hoped some day to film several episodes which would tell the story in depth. As a result of this first show, Ethel Anderson Becker, a Klondike historian, sent him dozens of E.A. Hegg photos taken in 1897 and 1898 at Chilkoot Pass and in the Yukon. Don became more eager to research the topic.

E.A. Hegg, an adventurous photographer from Bellingham, Washington, joined the stampede to the gold fields of the Klondike. But the gold Hegg planned to find was in the form of photographs of one of the most amazing human stories in history, where tens of thousands of people, penniless from the depression that gripped the nation, endured untold hardships to get to the Klondike near Dawson, where gold had been found in abundance.

In 1969, Don got his chance to delve into this story. The *Exploration Northwest* crew planned to retrace the trail to the Klondike by hiking the Chilkoot Pass. They filmed two half-hour shows telling about that part of the epic saga. When the shows aired in October 1969, fan mail flooded in. One viewer, Mrs. John Preston, sent to Don a family diary written by Fanny Ostrander during the gold rush as she accompanied her husband to the Yukon.

The next summer, the *Exploration Northwest* crew returned to where they ended their hike on the Canadian side of the Chilkoot Pass and filmed three more half-hour shows canoeing 540 miles down the Yukon River to Dawson, arriving in time to film the annual Discovery Days Celebration.

When Don and I were beginning our life together, he and the *Exploration Northwest* crew were filming on the Chilkoot Pass. I remember vividly that they were at the summit of Chilkoot Pass when Apollo 11 landed on the moon—a reminder of the tremendous jump in technology in less than a century.

In 1971, Don used the Hegg photos and the Ostrander diary, along with quotes from the "bard of the north," Robert Service, stills taken on the KOMO film trip on Chilkoot Pass, and information from

Murray Morgan's book about Hegg's Klondike experiences, *One Man's Gold Rush*, to begin writing a "then-and-now" book telling of the hardships endured by the Klondikers hiking the Chilkoot Pass in winter. He titled his manuscript "Trail to the Klondike."

Don was a writer, not a businessman. Although he finished the initial draft of the manuscript in one year, he never really tried to find a publisher. Occasionally throughout the next twenty years he worked on the manuscript for this book.

In 1993, his brief struggle with cancer interrupted his writing, a struggle that he met by often quoting Ethel Anderson Becker: "We all have our Chilkoots to climb." He would not live to see the final product.

Following Don's death, just three months after being diagnosed with pancreatic cancer, my sister, Carolyn Street LaFond, a freelance writer in Olympia, Washington, remembered the unpublished manuscript on the Klondike gold rush in Don's desk drawer written two decades earlier.

While helping me cope with all the details of Don's sudden death, she also formatted the Klondike manuscript on disk and began contacting publishers. As a writer, she had been entranced with the manuscript when Don first showed it to her. She recognized its uniqueness and noted that the Klondike centennial was approaching. Through Carolyn's efforts, the manuscript found a home at Washington State University Press.

This, then, is a living memorial to Don's twenty-year project, with admiration from his sister-in-law and me.

Linda McCune
Woodinville, Washington
January 1997

Chapter One

Ghosts

To those of us who have trod its trails and listened to the whisper of its silent voices, the Klondike gold rush, which marked the turn of the last century, needs no curtain call to fame. Like others of its kind, promulgated on hope and charged with a hard-fisted frontier desperation, it was a period of timeless vitality, of horizons stretched and expanded.

The same restlessness stirred Robert Service as he roamed the ramshackle streets of Dawson, "a solitary dreamer" gathering inspiration for his poetic musings from the rapidly declining capital of the Klondike. "Ghosts were all about me, whispering and pleading in the mystic twilight."

Decades later, they're still there. Perhaps not in ethereal form, although I wouldn't go on record as disputing that possibility. But certainly, more tangible specters were left behind. Having rubbed shoulders with the dispossessed, one cannot lightly brush aside the evidence of their passing.

Today, they stare at you from the vacant windows of abandoned settlements: Hootelinqua, Fort Selkirk, Forty Mile. Old telegraph stations, deserted Indian villages, and Mounted Police posts stand as rotting bookmarks to the past. The same specters haunt the skeletal remains of miners' cabins scattered along the creeks and tributaries which feed the broad channel of the Yukon River. This same, strong artery that once carried miners to the gold fields now flows strangely

Opposite: *The Dawson waterfront in 1899.*

silent through the land. Yet the land remains the same. The well-publicized topography, which gave rise to the works of Robert Service and the likes of Sam McGee, still reflects the ice-locked legacy of the north country. And Dawson, surrounded by weed-grown tailing piles and defunct dredges, is still the undisputed Queen of the Klondike.

Once the magic of Dawson echoed over the whistling storm-blasts of the Chilkoot and White Pass summits, as an army of fortune seekers struggled north. They had heard it again in the roar of Whitehorse Rapids and Miles Canyon. And by the summer of '98, Dawson had become a sawboard Shangri-La, squatting on the mud flats of the Klondike and smelling of gold.

They called it Dawson, but it could just as well have been Crede or Virginia City, or any of its notorious predecessors, all of which had been designed to handle the gold while assuaging frustrations of the average miner. Located on the Canadian side of the border, Dawson was subject to the ministrations of the Royal Northwest Mounted Police. But beyond that, those early mining towns were all sisters under the skin, ready to embrace the greenhorn and relieve him of his money at any hour of the day or night. Prompted by months of abstinence and by generous effusions of local liquor, it was an oasis; a bawdy slattern in carnival dress whose voice was the screech of fiddles, the rattle of poker chips, and the foot-stomping hilarity and blandishments of Lousetown across the river.

A man could buy a bottle, a bath, or a woman. He could get his dandruff removed, his eyebrows lifted, or his teeth knocked out. He could also get them filled with souvenir nuggets which, as far as most of them were concerned, were as close to the gold as they would get anyway. Not that there wasn't plenty of gold around! Looking up Eldorado Creek, the stampeder could feast his eyes on the richest valley in the Klondike. Four solid miles of muck, tailing piles, sluice boxes, and shafts—and not a single blank claim on its entire length.

3

Eldorado and Hunker Creek both rose above the Ridge, a chain of hills overlooked by a promontory called the Dome. Then there was Bonanza, or Rabbit Creek, the sorry-looking moose pasture where George Carmack and his Indian brothers-in-law, Skookum Jim and Tagish Charlie, had inadvertently stumbled upon the Klondike's first rich strike in August 1896. It was the place where Robert Henderson, the Canadian prospector, had told Carmack it might be. The south side of the Ridge gave rise to Dominion, Sulphur, and Quartz creeks, and all were contained within a swampy, pasture-rolling land of low crests. The creeks scrolled through in patterns of their own, sometimes weaving around the paystreak, occasionally crossing it, but more often than not missing it altogether. Rarely was the paystreak near the surface and the only way to find it was to dig for it.

Poor man's mining, they called it. And so it was. Alternately firing at night to thaw the frozen ground and digging during the day, it took a month to reach bedrock and weeks more to drift for the paystreak. "Luck," they said. "Cards, pinballs, or bedrock, it was all the same." Luck! "A man could dig all year with nothing to show for it, while ten feet away on another claim, they could be picking out nuggets bigger than the other fella's calluses."

During the long, hard winters when the men on the creeks died of scurvy, Dawson kept jigging to a ragtime tune and drinking Tex Richard's watered-down Rye. When seven men froze to death on a stampede to Swede's Creek, "Swiftwater" Bill Gates, the town's leading lothario, bought Gussie Lamore a new hat to cheer her up. A fetching creation of satin and feathered plumes, it set him back $275. Even at sixty below zero, gold had a marvelous, warm color.

By fall, the Bering Sea and Yukon River were frozen and miners had to wait until summer of 1897 to take their gold out of the region.

Opposite: *Preparing for the ascent of Chilkoot Pass, spring 1898.*

Prospectors preparing for ascent
of Chilkoot Pass - Spring of 1898

En route to Klondike Gold Fields

605

5

As the steamboat *Portland* approached Puget Sound, telegraph reports came streaming in from the outlying ports that a boat with a "ton of gold" was about to arrive at the docks on Elliot Bay in Seattle. The date was July 17, 1897.

The *Seattle Post-Intelligencer* first scooped the story with Erastus Brainerd's report of the steamboat's cargo. The headlines read, **"Gold! Gold! Gold! 68 Rich Men On The Steamer 'Portland'! Stacks Of Yellow Metal!"** When the boat docked, it was met by nearly every inhabitant of Seattle. Sixty-eight miners disembarked the *Portland,* and with them their crates of gold.

The hysteria in Seattle began immediately. The mayor and police chief resigned. Ministers left their churches and a newspaper lost all its reporters. The whole town was Klondike crazy and it spread quickly across the United States. By the end of the day, the *Portland* was booked to capacity for a return trip to Dawson. Other derelict boats were pressed into service.

Back in the Midwest, *The Chicago Tribune*'s big story opened with the words, "Gold in Seattle today is measured by the hundred pounds. The 'Portland' is here from the Klondike and has brought a treasure weighing more than a ton!" Actually, the cargo manifest listed closer to two tons, but who was to quibble? A "ton" was enough to trigger the flood, and in the months that followed, it became a torrent fed by many streams. Frantic people rushed northward jammed together in the holds of creaking ships. The little steamship *Amur* had room for sixty passengers, yet she managed to squeeze in five hundred. Leaky tubs were manned by crews who had never heard of tide rips or the churning waters that tore at the Alaska coast line. Many people lost their lives. The year 1898 held the record, averaging three shipwrecks a month. Yet nothing could stop this human torrent.

Opposite: *Front Street Seattle in the 1890s.*

FRONT ST.
SEATTLE.
No. 97.

7

By fall of 1897, 10,000 people had passed through Seattle. An estimated 100,000 headed to the Yukon within the next year. Enterprising businesses in Seattle quickly responded to supply the would-be miner with provisions. The Royal Canadian Mounted Police had set stringent requirements for people entering the Yukon. Survival was tough in this frozen region and the RCMP would not allow anyone to enter without a year's worth of provisions. Many a Klondiker owed his life to the diligence of the RCMP.

The traditional access to the interior of the Yukon and the Klondike was the all-water route by way of the Pacific Ocean, the Bering Sea, and the Yukon River. However, the ice-clogged Bering was navigable only a few months out of the year. Passage was scarce and expensive. The alternate route was more direct, albeit more difficult. The two most widely used trails to the Klondike began at the northern end of Alaska's Inside Passage. Both could be reached from established ports of embarkation on the West Coast: Seattle, Tacoma, Port Townsend, Victoria, B.C., and to a lesser degree, Portland and San Francisco. Both trails converged at Lake Bennett, which formed the headwaters of the navigable Yukon on the Canadian side of the border. From this point, the stampeders could complete their journey downriver to Dawson and the gold fields.

Like everything else, it looked good on paper. The problem, of course, was making it work. The White Pass, at 2,900 feet, was lower than Chilkoot and, in theory, purported to be an all-weather route open to pack animals and even wagons. Unfortunately, at the beginning of the stampede, this proved to be untrue and by the fall of '97, 3,000 dead horses lined the trail. The Chilkoot, at least, was a trail; an old Indian trail which started at Dyea, a small settlement consisting of some 250 Chilkat Indians and a trading post owned by Healy and Wilson. It was also the nearest route from tidewater to the head of navigation. Complicating this passage, however, was a 3,600 foot summit, windswept and bathed in almost continual fog.

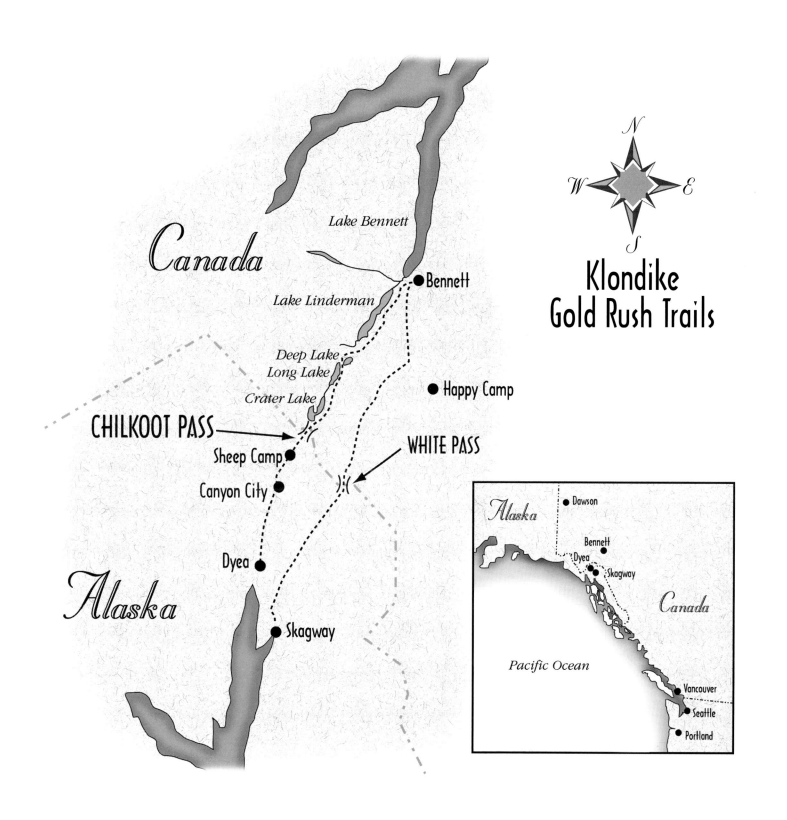

Lake Bennett

Canada

Bennett

Lake Linderman

Deep Lake
Long Lake

Happy Camp

Crater Lake

CHILKOOT PASS

WHITE PASS

Sheep Camp

Canyon City

Dyea

Alaska

Skagway

N
W *E*
S

Klondike
Gold Rush Trails

Alaska

Dawson

Bennett

Dyea

Skagway

Canada

Pacific Ocean

Vancouver

Seattle

Portland

For the vast majority of stampeders who elected to follow this overland link, the Chilkoot and White Pass trails became a cruel test of resolve in which 100,000 people participated and, as near as can be determined, 40,000 completed—22,000 via the Chilkoot Pass alone! By the time most of these reached the gold fields, there were no claims left to be staked. Most money made during the Klondike stampede was made by the suppliers. "Mine the Miners" was their motto. Most miners spent all they had on supplies and transportation.

Today, since the White Pass also serves as the route for the White Pass and Yukon Railway, it is the one most often seen. Many of the early Klondikers timed their trip to coincide with the completion of the railroad which, by 1899, had reached as far as Lake Bennett. The Chilkoot, as a result, is left to the more durable breed of hiker who, for his efforts, can view close-hand the ruins and artifacts still scattered along its entire length.

A century after the rush the Chilkoot Pass remains a dramatic symbol of the Klondike gold rush, still strewn with the discarded litter of the human tidal wave that once briefly engulfed it. It is here, more than anywhere else on the Trail of '98, that one encounters the spirits of the dispossessed: the flutter of an old magazine in the wind, a strand of rusted cable, the remains of a sled—crushed now by the weight of uncounted snows—a woman's high-laced shoe wedged between rocks at the base of the pass. Moving through this forlorn mosaic, there is a tendency to listen for silent voices. Half-formed images play like shadows across the mind. Imagination? Yes. But beyond that, a brooding presence, as if the play had ended but the curtain had yet to come down.

Trail Street, Dyea.

Opposite: *Looking north along Main Street in Dyea.*

Chapter Two

On The Trail

Heading the White Pass, at the end of Lynn Canal, was Skagway, billed as "Gateway to the Gold Fields." But as far as Skagway was concerned, the gold was in the pockets and "pokes" of the migrating miners. The Klondike lay miles away.

For the stampeders, Skagway was the first contact with the north. The town hasn't changed much. Visitors still delight in prowling the weather-beaten boardwalks and rubbing shoulders with the old trail town's historic ghosts. As usual, the lion's share of attention still goes to Jefferson Randolph "Soapy" Smith, whose nefarious activities once alarmed the stampeders so much they started bypassing the town. The local merchants eventually eradicated his "roadblock" in a celebrated shoot-out which took place on the town's docks. The duel between Soapy Smith and Frank Reid, a member of the vigilante committee, proved fatal to both gentlemen. They were buried on the outskirts of Skagway in what has come to be known as the Gold Rush Cemetery. Today, one encounters the mystique of these historic landmarks on "The Gold Rush Trail," held over and nurtured these many years.

Cameraman Bill Bacon, film editor Joel Schroedel, and director Tim Bullard, take time out to "rub shoulders" with Skagway.

The impressive marker belongs to Frank Reid...

...but it is the bad man Jefferson "Soapy" Smith they remember the most!

Opposite: *More than a thousand lots sold almost immediately as Skagway sprang up during the rush.*

From this seaport terminus of the White Pass and Yukon Railway, the ribbons of steel point north to the interior of the Yukon. (The railroad's builder, Mike Heney, once laid the tracks through Skagway under cover of darkness over the objections of the city fathers.) By 1898, Skagway's city limits extended four miles up the canyon with a population, including the transient hordes, fluctuating from 15,000 to 20,000. At the time of our filming in 1969, the residency stood at a scant 700. However, with tourism now rivaling the railroad as the town's principal industry, the Eagle's Hall still echoes the sound of old-time music and the stamp of dancing feet. Visitors from places like Mason City, Iowa, and Sioux Falls, South Dakota, revel in the faded reflection of what used to be the most wide-open town on the trail to the Klondike.

Looming in Skagway's horizon at the time of our visit was a proposed Klondike Gold Rush National Historical Park (now in place), a joint effort of Canada and the United States. A section of historical and recreational zones would extend from Lynn Canal to Dawson, including Skagway's historical district, the abandoned townsite of Dyea, and the White Pass and Chilkoot trails.

Skagway at the time of our visit, from a vantage point that was not available to the Klondike photographers. We took this shot from the air coming in to land on the small, graveled landing strip which serves as a runway.

On the morning after our arrival, rain clouds awaited. We would see them the next time at the top of the pass.

Opposite: *Skagway's wharves.*

SKAGUAY WHARVES.

303.a
H&S

15

Four miles up the beach from Skagway and separated by a mountain ridge was the beginning of another trail. Called the Chilkoot, it would absorb the first movement through the forbidding mountains that screened the coast from the interior of the Yukon. At the head of Chilkoot trail lay the town of Dyea, which expired quite some time ago.

Fearing the dangerous tidal bore that existed, ship captains dropped anchor in the open sea and the hapless Klondikers had to struggle ashore as best they could. Canadian authorities, concerned that the stampeders would overtax the Yukon's meager supplies, had ruled that each man had to bring enough to last a year. Bales of hay, drums of kerosene, lumber, barrels of whiskey—whatever would float they threw overboard on the in-going tide. Horses, sheep, dogs, and any other livestock the vessels carried were also dumped into the icy water and forced to swim for it. In time, the beachline took on the appearance of a toppling wall; a confused mix of bags, sacks, and stacks of abused property. Some of it was water-soaked and much of it burst open; angry owners had to identify it any way possible. Tent space was at a premium, and men camped wherever they could. Some, forgetting about the tide, awoke to find the whole mess back in the water again!

Three quarters of a century after the gold rush, rotted piling still march in ragged precision across the tideflats. We looked in vain for some time-worn article that might have been left behind.

Opposite: *Each miner had to have enough supplies to last a year before entering Canada. Tons of freight entered Dyea, waiting to be packed to the gold fields.*

For the first ten miles, the Chilkoot trail followed the Taiya River, crossing it from side to side about every 200 yards. In summer, it was possible to freight the outfit in canoes, but this required considerable skill against the current. Consequently, most Klondikers used horses, or carts (many which they pulled themselves), or packed their gear on their backs. But whether a man used his own back or a Chilkat Indian's (residents of the place), all gear had to be moved forward in relays with partners.

Something about the nature of the undertaking dwarfed the spirit. Gone now was the camaraderie of shipboard life. Single file: horse to horse, sled to sled, and raft to raft; from this point on, every minute counted. Every minute and every ounce! Not an extra spoon, photograph, or yard of rope went over the trail than the bearer was willing to carry. By fall of 1897, a sea of tents, rough board saloons, shacks, and stores already covered the Indian village of Dyea as newly arrived merchants hurried to create a makeshift metropolis for the thousands pouring ashore. Skagway experienced the same frenzy, but Dyea enjoyed a temporary advantage. By February of '98, *The Dyea Trail*, a weekly publication, reported that "people who had been away for three weeks were astonished at the number of new buildings"; that "there wasn't a vacant lot for three miles up the river!"; that "the Dyea Hotel [one of seven] featured a full orchestra and business was crushing." At other times it noted, "The steamer, *Clara*, had blown up off

At the time of our journey, it was as though Dyea had never existed. Buildings had collapsed. Where Trail Street's dance halls and gambling dens roared and prospered, there was only silence. Where once trampling crowds fought for space to pitch a tent, there was room to spare.

Opposite: *Dyea in 1898.*

DYEA, ALASKA

19

Seward City with loss of 75 lives"; "four companies of troops were being sent to preserve order"; "1,200 people had landed the previous week"; "the trail was in splendid condition." It also stated, "day after day, it became plainer that the only avenue into the goldfields was by way of Dyea!" a rosy prediction deflated when construction began on the White Pass and Yukon Railway and the tide changed in favor of Skagway. Dyea's population, well over 3,000, rapidly declined. Its numerous hotels, stores, and banks were vacated and in a few short years it became a true ghost town.

A surprising number of women braved the rigors of "Old Chilkoot." An article in *The Dyea Trail* referred to a "plucky little woman dressed in a mackinaw suit and pulling a sled load of goods who attracted considerable attention on the trail this week. Each day she made a trip or two to the waterfront, returning with several hundred pounds on her sleigh. She asked assistance from no one and attended strictly to the business of getting her outfit up the trail to her cache. The woman is Mrs. Anna K. Smith of Tacoma. She is thoroughly equipped and will endeavor to be one of the first to reach Dawson in the spring."

From left to right: the author, Don McCune, host and narrator of Exploration North-west; *Lyle Kleinschmidt, motel owner and fellow Klondike "buff"; Gerry ter Haar, a Dutch photographer; Bill Bacon,* Exploration Northwest *cameraman; and Tim Bullard, who directed the show. This was the crew who made the trek. Joel Schroedel, the other member, was assigned the responsibility of handling the aerial photography.*

The trail sign located near the steel bridge that crosses the Dyea River (known as "The Taiya") told the story. From here to Lake Linderman was twenty-seven miles. For us it was a one-way trip, but one we would never forget.

Opposite: Despite the gallantry displayed by one slightly overburdened Klondiker, stream crossings were usually made the hard way. Some women made the trip to the gold fields, such as these dressed in Victorian travel attire and identified as Irene Stanley, May Biggs, Maude Earl (being ferried), Lulu Johnson, and Mrs. Jack Sullivan. Lulu Johnson later drowned on the Sophia.

Above the delta of the Taiya River, the trail extended north between sharply rising mountains. From that point to the summit, it was mostly up. When the poet Joaquin Miller arrived in the summer of '97 and offered to make a quick reconnaissance of the gold rush, his first dispatch read, "Truly, if this had been my own woods on the 'Hights,' the scene could not have been more pretty! The cottonwoods moaned and groaned, water came tumbling down wooded valleys and my boots became yellow for the many blossoms reaching my knees. A prettier walk than I found there on the banks of that swift stream could not be found in the United States!" Apparently, he did not notice the men tramping beside him, for he never mentioned them. Nor did he say anything about the dead horses and blowflies, or mosquitoes and sump holes. He also avoided the subject of the river's pollution although, like everyone else, he must have used it for drinking water.

Since the original trail follows the right bank of the Taiya River, we elected to cross by hand-operated cable car, thus saving ourselves several miles of rough going—a luxury not enjoyed by those who had preceded us in years past.

Tim Bullard balances on a skinny tree as Johnny O'Daniel, our guide, and Gerry ter Haar look on. As one veteran Klondiker explained it: "A man carrying his food, his cooking utensils and working tools on his back has no time nor disposition to cut down trees. When he comes to an unfrozen stream, he wades it, or if a tree has fallen across, so much the better."

"After five miles of road, all hell begins!" reported a British officer. The terrain was a rough, wooded tangle of hemlock, spruce, and cottonwood. The hooves of pack animals quickly chewed the trail into a quagmire. To stay on it was to risk bogging down; to leave was to fight through clutching branches or to risk a fall on wet rock. Some eight miles from Dyea, the trail dropped down again to skirt the edge of the river. Here the Klondiker caught his first glimpse of the snowfields which marked the approach of the pass, a sobering spectacle for those who now found the Chilkoot taking on certain nightmarish qualities not apparent in the first flush of enthusiasm. At this point, they could still use pack animals; horses, if they had them, or dogs, many that had been commandeered off some city street and were usually ill-equipped in size or disposition. Here again, a partner could make a difference. While one went back for another load, the other could make camp and prepare the evening meal, usually coffee, beans, and biscuits.

Johnny O'Daniel, resident of Skagway, had made the trip a number of times and was helpful in pointing out locations and landmarks for the camera.

In addition to his seventy-five pound pack, Bill Bacon also carried the Aeroflex camera.

The basic food list for the trip over the trail generally included: 500 pounds of flour, 200 pounds of bacon, 100 pounds each of sugar, beans, dried fruit, and potatoes, and 50 pounds of corn meal, rolled oats, and rice. To this they added 48 2-pound cans of corned beef, 30 pounds of lard, 36 yeast cakes, 25 pounds of coffee, 5 pounds of cocoa, 48 large cans of condensed milk, 25 pounds of salt and pepper, plus 200 extra pounds of cornmeal and fat bacon for the dogs.

Just as important was the hardware a miner needed to build a boat or cabin, to sink timbers in a mine, to erect a windlass, or to build a rocker and sluice boxes. If he carried a medicine chest, it might contain cathartic pills, liniment, tincture of iron (for the blood), extract of Jamaican ginger (for the stomach), laudanum, bandages, surgeon's lint and sponge, belladonna plasters, chloroform, and quinine capsules. Most brought tobacco; a few had books.

We paused for lunch in an area closely resembling many E.A. Hegg photos. Hot coffee? Yes. Beans? No. Freeze-dried food. Even with us, weight was crucial.

On the Taiya there were some clouds but still enough skyline to see part of the glacier.

Opposite: *Many stampeders bought dogs to take with them as sled-pullers, companions, and, as a last resort, meat.*

Nine miles from Dyea, in the shelter of Dyea Canyon, Canyon City took shape. "City" was a misnomer. Canyon City was simply the first camp between Dyea and the pass, a logical stopover for the massive relay of equipment and supplies. As time went on, space became a premium and the "city" offered little in the way of creature comforts. One Klondiker described "the dyspeptic belch of a stampeding prospector who had eaten heartily of baking powder biscuits, the explosive little white beans and pork. Fourteen of these volcanic human beings packed into a 10 by 12 cabin. It got so hot the stench of a sawdust-covered beer joint was a thousand times more inviting. Somebody opened the door to get a breath of fresh air and 20 dogs moved in!"

Through this canyon they hauled boats and knockdown sawmills. Greenhorns, fresh off the streets, pushed frail two-wheel carts and wheelbarrows; anything that would get them closer to the gold fields.

Back home, optimism progressed from semi-controlled to unrestrained. People were telling themselves that Klondike nuggets were big as hen's eggs. The governor of Canada's Northwest Territories stated that he "believed the real mass of gold wealth was still untouched" with fully 9,000 miles of golden waterways waiting to be prospected.

We had planned to overnight at the Canyon City shelter but found it was already occupied by a trail crew. The remains of Canyon City itself are located across the river.

Here the Taiya posed more of a problem. The bridge needed replacing. Following a brief session with a sharp ax felling our own makeshift bridge, we "tight-roped" across minus packs and wondered if we would be able to make it back to pick them up again.

This ancient boiler had been used to generate electricity for what had once been Canyon City.

Opposite: *Canyon City—the first camp between Dyea and Chilkoot Pass.*

29

And so they continued to come. Farmers, butchers, college boys, barbers, milk cart drivers, policemen, politicians, stable hands, newspaper reporters, graybeards, and striplings; theirs was now the grim reality of the trail. Many had pawned all their possessions to get here, leaving behind families forced to exist as best they could. During the long months to come, some would be lost in the foaming frenzy of Miles Canyon and Whitehorse Rapids. Some would die of scurvy when, with grub running low, they burrowed like moles in the frozen gravel, blind to all but the golden temptress who now ruled their lives. Ahead of them, the fog-shrouded hills gave promise of tomorrow's toil, while behind them, an army was forming.

Back home, it had been easy to throw in an extra sweater, a padlock, or some luxury. Now, when life itself depended on what each man brought in, it was wise to listen to those with Yukon experience. The greenhorn learned to compare outfits, to pick up pointers from the old-timers.

Was the outfit absolutely basic: sled, tent, air-tight stove, blankets, plenty of beans? Did he have enough mosquito netting? If he didn't, he'd better have! Who would believe mosquitoes could kill a dog, gathering so thickly on the hide and fur of an animal they almost covered it from view? Back in Dyea, mosquito netting cost $5 a yard, yet summertime travel was impossible without it.

Rotted power poles, cross bars, and metal braces mark the site of a former power line at Canyon City. No glass insulators, however. We looked but could find none.

A few old structures remained, but most of Canyon City is gone. Sod roofs eventually gave way on the log cabins and, once exposed to the elements, the walls collapsed.

Not a soul around. It was here at Canyon City that we began to feel the closeness with the past, as though whatever had been here was just ahead of us.

Opposite: *Canyon City.*

During the winter, he needed black glasses to guard against snow blindness. Citric acid warded off scurvy. How about liniment? Candles? What could he leave behind? Did he need two frying pans? How much soap? Was he going it alone or did he have a partner? Many things would serve them both and help lighten the load.

Aside from the weight, there was also the matter of duty. Canadian duty. Thirty percent on ammunition! Thirty-five percent on edge tools! Flour was twenty percent! And the Mounties awaited at the top of the pass.

Thirteen miles up the river, a cleft in the canyon opened into Sheep Camp, so-named by hunters who had established headquarters in the windswept valley many years before. There was but one exit, the pass itself. The Taiya River drained the snowfields nearby and the sparsely forested slopes provided the last fuel on the western side of the divide. It was also the last place offering bed and board.

We had camped the night before on the river and the first day had taken its toll with blisters and sore muscles. For some of us, the trek also brought an agonizing reappraisal of what we had thought important enough to bring along.

We started to see the first signs of what I chose to think of as "The Chilkoot Mosaic": discarded personal debris on the trail itself.

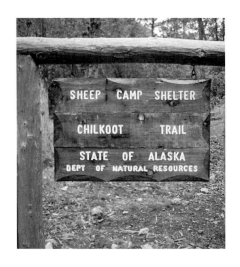

The February 18, 1898 edition of *The Dyea Trail* published a scathing editorial, along with an account of conditions at Sheep Camp. Men, weary of waiting for the law to act—and what law there was, was grossly inefficient or had been bought off by Soapy Smith who had reached Skagway just before winter closed that port in 1897—decided to take the law into their own hands. A self-appointed committee tried two men for stealing another man's outfit. One, who tried to escape when he was pursued, committed suicide. The other was flogged and sent back to Dyea wearing a sign, "Thief, Pass Him Along." Complaints were sworn out for the men who had done the flogging, but they had "gotten over the summit and down to Bennett on the Canadian side."

"Notwithstanding the fact that citizens of Sheep Camp, as well as along the trail, have been annoyed by thieves, we are not living in the age of witch craft and barbarianism, but in a peaceful, law-abiding community," railed the editorial. "Tis not the bruise that galls but the blush. Let us have justice and justice to all."

Trail shelters are well-marked and maintained on both sides of border, such as this one at Sheep Camp.

As far as accommodations were concerned, this was it until we got to Linderman. Unlike the shelter at Canyon City, the Sheep Camp shelter was available. However, on this second day out we planned to make it as far as The Scales at the foot of the pass. It was with some reluctance that we scratched Sheep Camp off our overnight list and proceeded on.

Opposite: Sheep Camp was the last place before the pass offering bed and board. This soon became a city of 7,000 to 8,000 stampeders, complete with telegraph lines.

Even today, the Chilkoot has a way of grinding you down to size. What we couldn't know, of course, was the mood of desperation which frequently added to our predecessors' exhaustion—those who carried burdens besides the ones of the trail: emotional, physical, financial. Treading on the heels of thousands already ahead, they feebly grasped at the glory, never knowing what hour would mark the end, what minute would find them stumbling back, "gnawing at the black crust of defeat." 🐾

Me absorbing a little atmosphere!

Sometimes the best camera angle is from the supine position!

"OK, men, on your feet! We'll never make it sitting here!"

Opposite: *I've often wondered if the "Exhausted Stampeder" who served as the unsuspecting model for E.A. Hegg ever awakened to the fact that he had carved his own peculiar niche in the Klondike Hall of Fame by falling asleep.*

EXHAUSTED STAMPEDER

Chapter Three

The Ascent

By October of '97, the first snow of winter began to cover the trail, lessening the burden of transporting supplies. In winter Klondikers could sled 400 pounds in one load. Some sleds were pulled by dogs, horses, or oxen. One man had a team of goats! But the majority were pulled by hand using manpower and, occasionally, even womanpower.

The Klondike story is filled with several accounts of women working right along with their men. One poor woman carried a babe-in-arms the entire distance from Dyea to Dawson, a labor of love which ended tragically when the baby sickened and died after reaching the gold fields.

Notes from the diary of Fanny Ostrander who, in 1897, accompanied her husband across the Chilkoot Pass, describe the conditions encountered.

> Yesterday, we walked from Canyon City to Sheep Camp and met and passed all kinds of people, some with great packs upon their backs, others with dog teams and packhorses, and still others who, like ourselves, were less burdened. As we neared Sheep Camp an old man was making coffee outside his tent. He invited us to rest and have a cup, which we gladly did. It was the first instance of miner's hospitality. As a rule, everyone here is looking after himself. On the trail this afternoon we saw one woman driving an ox hitched to a sled. Another was helping her husband pull a sled up the trail. Poor creatures, they will earn all they can get and I hope it amounts to thousands!

The winter then approaching the Yukon would soon turn it into a trough of ice; the passes would choke with blizzards. Thousands of climbers were already on their way or preparing to leave before the situation became critical. Back in the States, Secretary of the Interior Cornelius N. Bliss issued a public warning to those attempting to get to Alaska, urging them to postpone their trip until the following spring. He cautioned them of the possible consequences should they be detained in the frozen wilderness where no relief could reach, however great the need.

Of the many thousands who took to the trails in 1897, no one reached Dawson before freeze-up and the traffic jammed and swelled like a dammed-up river. A late storm added two feet of wet snow to the summit of Chilkoot Pass. The prudent withdrew to a safer position and Sheep Camp became a welter of struggling men, howling dogs, and abandoned horses. Telegraph lines had been strung from Dyea but high winds and snow hampered maintenance.

In the spring, the army prepared to move once again, and here in this last staging area before the assault on the summit, Fanny Ostrander wrote in her diary.

> **April 13, 1898:** Last night the wind blew a perfect gale! I was afraid the poor old shack of a hotel would go. Sitting here in my room I can look through the big cracks in the floor to the kitchen below. I just heard one man in the kitchen say to another that he had stuck close to school until he came to fractions. And then, by God, he quit as he could never get the hang of it. Next to our room is another room with about 25 bunks in it. It is occupied. We have to pass through this room to get to our meals past men in all stages of dress and undress.

Opposite: *Winter in the Chilkoot.*

April 14, 1898: Thursday finds us still at Sheep Camp. The weather is storming on the summit. We made a vain attempt this morning to get out but only traveled about a half mile and was turned back. I know our friends would have laughed to see us trudging along. John had a small valise which he carried on his pack and I followed right at his heels. I thought of the old Frenchman who lived in Olympia [Washington], and led his blind wife around. I did not mention it to John as he was not in a very cheerful frame of mind, owing to the tussle he had with his pack as it slipped on his back. Poor fellow. I hated to see him carry it knowing that if it hadn't have been for me he wouldn't have had to, as it is mostly my traps. In the meantime, Sheep Camp is a "cheap" place to stay with its several advantages.

From Sheep Camp to the summit four miles away, the trail bent sharply upward, winding over the shelves of ice during the winter and over slippery shale and granite boulders during the summer. The trail itself, such as it was, had been built by the Chilkat Indians, who had used it effectively as a means of controlling trade and ensuring revenue from the neighboring tribes.

The word "Chilkoot" means to pack or carry, a synonym we found increasingly worrisome.

Looking back, I figure the Chilkat Indians had called it pretty close. We were packing a "white man's burden," averaging between seventy and seventy-five pounds, including camera gear and film, and found it was all we could handle.

Opposite: *After Sheep Camp the trail ascended sharply and many miners employed Chilkat Indians to help them to the summit.*

Broad-shouldered and physically powerful, the Chilkat could handle tremendous loads, up to 100 pounds for the men, with the women frequently handling a "white man's burden" of seventy-five. With the arrival of the Klondikers, they hired out as packers to anyone who could pay the price, a fairly modest twelve cents a pound to begin with. By the end of the season it had risen to thirty-eight cents. And this was for conveniently proportioned bundles. Stoves were higher, as were pianos and other less manageable objects, all of which seemed to find their way over the pass as the occasion demanded. On what became known as the "Poor Man's Pass," few Klondikers could pay the Indians' price or, for that matter, the half as much charged for the use of a horse.

From Sheep Camp, the trail twined off into tracks that struggled upward toward what had become known as The Scales, for it was there that the packs were weighed, and the packer's price increased. It was located at the foot of the pass.

During the summer, the Klondiker faced a cliff of sliding rocks. The rest of the year it was ice, but summer or winter, it stood there like an impregnable jaw, capable of wrath and punishment. The burdened climbers, many physically unfit to begin with, picked up their first set of blisters after landing at Dyea. In relaying their supplies thirty-five miles to the head of navigation on the Yukon River, many would be forced to cover that distance fifty times and more before they managed to get their necessary supplies to the river. For them, the Chilkoot Pass

In places, it's almost straight up. Loose rock poses a hazard, especially to the man below.

It's bear country and Lyle Kleinschmidt carried a rifle. As it turned out, it was an unnecessary burden, and created an extra problem with customs.

Opposite: *Looking east from the summit of Chilkoot Pass. Case and Draper photograph.*

LOOKING BACK FROM THE SUMMIT

CHILKOOT PASS ROUTE

316

CASE & DRAPER

45

became a symbol of their weakness and frustration, a malevolent thing girded by giant boulders and sheer glaciers—the most massive reaching down from a 2,000 foot ledge. Like the others, it hung there above the rocky defile. In the stillness of the night, the climbers could hear it grinding forward invisibly, a pebble or a boulder at a time. And what the glaciers didn't dislodge, flash floods did. Two boulders had been dubbed the "Stonehouses" by early arrivals because they were "each as big as a house." Spring floods rolled first one and then the other down into the river, and by 1899 they, too, had disappeared.

When our crew reached the pass in 1969, it was hard for us to believe that this slender scar across the jagged edge of the Sawtooths, which bore little resemblance to the pictures we had seen, was the famous Chilkoot! Surely time had dulled its teeth. Ravaged by uncounted storms, it had shrunk in size and significance.

Yet there were scattered ruins, including a few tramway supports still clinging doggedly to the far ridge—remains of a device constructed by a Tacoma company for those who could afford to pay to have their freight hauled up the summit rather than carrying it on their backs. And above all, there was that brooding presence. Almost against our will our fingers pried through the debris of the past—

Some of the tramway supports were still in place, enough, at least, for us to follow their progress along the steep ridgeline.

Scrambling to find a suitable place to unroll our sleeping bags, we surveyed our dwindling food supply with some misgiving. Food is always a major consideration whether it's in your belly or on your back! To pack it requires energy, and energy requires food.

Opposite: *View of the summit from The Scales, September 3, 1898.*

SUMMIT, FROM SCALES, CHILKOOT PASS.   SEPT 3, 1898.

47

searching for what, we didn't know. Affirmation, perhaps; something to indicate the degree of struggle. Pawing through bits and pieces that time had twisted into shapeless symbols, we came upon an old telegraph line connected to nowhere, with a sign reading "Local and Long Distance." Who would answer?

Surrounded by the spirits of the dispossessed, we heard again the whisper of silent voices. And looking up at that debris-strewn battlefield, we knew again that even when these remnants were gone, the struggle which had taken place here would never be erased.

From The Scales to the top of the pass, the Klondiker could take one of two routes. On the right the Peterson trail was less precipitous but longer. The left-hand route was the one normally taken. It was on this steep slope that steps were cut during the winter of '97, 1,200 by actual count. Klondikers would have the opportunity to count them many times over, a vicious and interminable treadmill which halted only at night and continued until each man had deposited the necessary tonnage at the top. Following one behind the other, it took from three to six hours to make the climb, the pace being set by the slowest. Those who dropped out of line waited until an opening again appeared.

On the morning of the third day, the fog came rolling up the canyon, heavy with rain. Nature had set the stage for what was to follow.

As far as we were concerned, it was a case of gilding the lily. The setting itself was eerie enough!

Opposite: *Many who looked up at the summit from this vantage point at The Scales simply gave up and turned back.*

On April 16 Fanny Ostrander recorded this account in her diary:

We had quite a rough hike over yesterday as it stormed hard most of the time. So nervous for fear of snowslides. It was terrifying to think that mountains of snow could let go and bury you. We could see very little ahead and it was well we couldn't as it would cause the bravest hearts to lose courage. At the last, it was almost straight up and down. Every few feet there were places to rest. John had cut a pole and I hung on to the pole and his coat tail. As we reached one of the places, a man who was resting said to his partner, "Well, By God! If it isn't enough to make a man lose his liver!" I looked up and laughed and then he added, "Yes, or a woman's!"

The long weeks on the trail and the jostling of too many human beings thrown together under intolerable conditions had begun to take their toll even among the strong. Drained by fatigue and dysentery, eyes red from the wind-blasts that swept the canyon, many climbers who looked up simply gave up. Tempers were short and there was bloodshed. And still the line kept moving—150 pounds, 200, 400, relay after relay, five miles forward, five miles back.

John Van Mehr's notes for March 11, 1898: "A week moving 4500 pounds five miles. River is frozen, dogs are wonderful, but we feel it. Damned hard work. H and R working #1 load ahead from here. I'm cook this camp and H next. R will take care of the dogs from here on. 17 below but don't seem that cold. Very clear."

Moving up, I clutched at strands of tramway cable dangling like some ancient lifeline anchored in the past but offering a false sense of security.

Along the trail we found the remains of a sled and part of an outfit.

Opposite: *The loaded sled to the right is being hauled up by the tram line—a conveyance few miners could afford. The dark streaks to the right of the packers are the trails made by stampeders on their slide down to the base of the mountain to get another load.*

207.   THE LAST CLIMB TO THE SUMMIT OF C⸺OT PASS.   COPYRIGHT 1898.   E.A.Hegg.

The entry for March 17 notes: "9 round trips to Sheep Camp, our second stop. Four blizzards. I'm working with Ray this week. Face all raw in spite of bacon grease and ashes. What I'd give to have a hot bath? Hah!"

On March 23 he wrote: "Nobody speaking on the trail. We move forward like dead men. Not even a howl out of the dogs. The Chilkoot is in front of us. The dogs are the only decent uncomplaining members of this party. R pulled his knife on me yesterday. Maybe I deserved it. This would be a hell of a place to be left. Would H bury me? I wonder."

On April 2 came this note: "We're going over tomorrow." Everything but their tent, stove, two days' provisions and the bedding had been freighted over the top.

"Ant-like, burdened, clinging in icy space," an estimated 22,000 Klondikers strained over the Chilkoot Pass between fall of '97 and spring of '98, like a human chain toiling toward the summit, the weaklings dropping behind.

The uncontrollably bad thing about winter was the weather. Howling gales were almost a daily occurrence. No matter how much a man bundled up, the wind reached in somewhere, tearing at fur and leather and penetrating sweaty bodies with an icy grip. When a climber was working, hauling, pushing, or packing, it was easy to perspire. And if he didn't change into dry clothing, his wet skin would freeze. Frostbite was common, leaving painful blisters and deep sores. Few Klondikers knew how to dress for the climate. Those who did

---

Leaving milepost 16 and heading up, we had the feeling that we were now one with the legions who had gone before.

The debris of the trail, including ice crampon.

Once an "Army of Fortune" faced this rocky defile in hope, hunger, and despair and found here the measure of the man.

wore an overall parka-like garment made of drill cloth which came below the knees and had a hood, usually fur-lined, that protected the face against the wind.

Pressed by time and dog-tired, meals became a spiritless project to be hurried through as quickly as possible. The monotonous bill of fare for most was half-cooked beans, whose prevalent pink color soon gave them the name "Alaska strawberries"—and dough cakes. The dough cakes were made by throwing a handful of snow into a sack of flour, adding salt and baking powder, stirring the mess into a ball, and dropping it into a skillet of bacon fat to fry. After eating and with the fire set for the night, the Klondiker would collect his cramped muscles and try to get some sleep.

Upon reaching the summit, the Klondikers deposited their provisions and gear in separate caches. It was a year's supply for an army, most of which had been purchased in Seattle at a time when the Queen City of the Northwest, still suffering from the effects of a disastrous fire, sorely needed an economic shot in the arm. For the average Klondiker, the fact that he had reached this far was a victory unto itself. Yet his journey had just begun. Dawson lay almost 600 miles away and what was not absolutely essential was discarded. Sleds, canoes, wagons, articles of clothing, cooking utensils, magazines, harnesses, boots, bottles, cans—anything that failed to make it in the final rush or, having served its purpose, no longer seemed necessary. In the years to come, this debris-laden pattern would trace the Klondikers' folly and glory with a woebegone eloquence. And having seen it, one is inclined to move along without disturbing the mosaic. 🐾

Winter comes early up here and stays late. It was July and pockets of snow still clung to the rocks as we approached the top of the pass. From sea level to summit, the Klondikers climbed over 3,700 feet.

Chapter Four

The Summit

The summit was windswept and bathed in almost continual fog. To get back down, the climbers used "The Grease Trail," worn down to a shoulder-high depth by thousands of sliding bodies. With the wind whistling in their ears, they breezed back to The Scales for another load. The race for the gold fields was on and the Chilkoot stood in the way!

The average stampeder carried from fifty to seventy-five pounds per trip. Professional packers averaged close to a hundred. An Indian once made it to the top with a 350-pound barrel, and a raw-boned Swede crawled up the icy slope with three four-by-six-inch timbers strapped to his back. The only sounds were the grunts and curses of the climbers, the creak of packs, the crunch of feet in the snow-packed trail, and the howl of the wind.

Noted John Van Mehr in his diary on April 10:

Easter Sunday! Stormy all week. Every kind of misery. This has been the most horrible month of my life. Left camp at 5 A.M. Clear for the first time. Made the top by 10 A.M. Slipped twice. God! Blue sky and sunshine here. Can see a lake below. Our troubles are over, thank God!

Ray was wonderful. He carried the dogs over, one at a time. Good Ray! Two trips to Hawley's and my one. I'm wondering why I'm alive today. Not because I've got guts.

Opposite: *The summit. A.C. Hirsch photograph.*

CHE on CHILCOOT SUMMIT *Alaska*

57

A note at the bottom of the page read, "We went to sleep in the sun. Woke up with snow falling like bullets all around us. In the blinding storm and darkness we were able to give the N.W.M.P. [Northwest Mounted Police] the go-by. Why not?"

When we ventured there in 1969, the summit still contained the evidence of the stampeders' travail, left behind for the wind to make music through the ribs of rope and rotten wood and dreams long dead. But for the *Exploration Northwest* party, the only terror the Chilkoot held was the prospect of starving before the evening meal was ready! Along with the normal ingredients, we fortified the stew with contributions from any and all, including two cans of Danish sausage, courtesy of Gerry ter Haar. Our cameraman Bill Bacon volunteered the tea, and Lyle Kleinschmidt supplied the cooking skill. We had brought grub enough for five days but already we were running short.

"The battlefield is silent where once they fought it out." But even now, one wonders if they would rise and follow again the clarion call of gold.

Where the stampeders suffered with weather and heavy loads, our major concern was finding enough ingredients for our evening stew.

Opposite: *E.A. Hegg had to carry bulky camera equipment over the pass. Despite the obstacles, his results frequently approached greatness, and this image is one of his best, showing the wind whipping the Canadian flag wildly over the Customs House. Once on top, the men could make use of sleds and dogs and in the foreground a Klondiker clutches his G-pole, with which he steers the sled as his team strains to move the heavy load toward Linderman, Bennett, and Dawson.*

SNOW STORM ON CHILKOOT SUMMIT COPYRIGHT 1898

The following morning we awakened to the sight of clouds heavy with rain. The weather, which had been threatening, had at last made up its mind. It was as if nature had decided to help set the stage for what was about to follow; a maneuver not in the script and one which director Tim Bullard had not called for. The setting was eerie enough. We had the feeling that we had somehow slipped back in time and were now one with the legions which had gone before.

As long as winter conditions prevailed, the pass at this point remained in fairly good condition. But in spring of '98 a late storm added to the snowpack and, during the heat of the day, the mountains echoed with the rumble of avalanches and snow slides. Stampeders were urged to do their packing at night when the trail was frozen and safe. The "cut-off," or Peterson Trail, to the right, was forbidden.

This bronze marker located near the summit pays tribute to the Klondike spirit which photographer E.A. Hegg captured so vividly in his famous picture of a "Snowstorm On The Summit."

Not far from the marker, we came upon the remains of a sled, flattened by the weight of uncounted storms and seventy-some winters. In the lower right-hand corner, hair still clings to the dog collar and scattered bones indicate the sled dogs died in their traces—and with them, possibly, the hopes of some Klondiker.

Opposite: *Scene of the snow slide on Chilkoot Pass that killed more than fifty Klondikers.*

AFTERMATH OF SNOW SLIDE ON CHILKOOT PASS

On April 3, 1898, tons of wet snow suddenly gave way and sluiced down the mountain burying several hundred stampeders who had ignored the advice. Most were able to claw their way out, but many were entombed alive. "I felt like I was in a plaster cast," reported one. "I thought of home, friends, every act of my life. Near me I could hear people moaning and praying, then I lost consciousness. When I awoke, I found myself on the floor of the tramway power house. They told me I had been buried for three hours." For many, however, the Chilkoot was slow to forgive. Despite frantic rescue efforts, the final death toll reached fifty-six. Their last resting place is the Slide Cemetery along the trail near Dyea. For these, the gold rush was over. For the others, the long trail waited.

Moving on, the survivors would take with them the memory of the ordeal and leave behind the incontestable evidence of hardship, including the bones of their dead, both animal and human.

"This is the Law of the Yukon that only the strong shall thrive, that surely weak shall perish and only the fit survive." 🐾

"I wanted the gold and I sought it; I hurled my youth into a grave." A last resting place, the Slide Cemetery along the trail near Dyea. For these the gold rush was over. For the others, the long trail awaited—the terrible Chilkoot and beyond.

Opposite: *Fifteen minutes after the snow slide, fifteen hundred men were on the scene digging out stampeders. They managed to rescue seven.*

Klondikers are shown ascending the summit of Chilkoot Pass. This most famous of all Hegg photographs, taken during the winter of 1898, made headlines all over the world. The dark line of stampeders, etched against a solid backdrop of white, became for all time the symbol of that great, human adventure that transformed the north country.

As winter wore on, the heavy snows covered the cache on the summit in deepening layers. Each small mountain of supplies was marked with a long pole to enable owners to find them again.

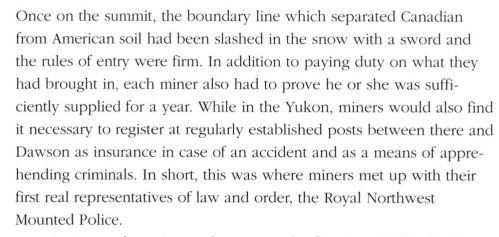

Chapter Five

The Descent

Once on the summit, the boundary line which separated Canadian from American soil had been slashed in the snow with a sword and the rules of entry were firm. In addition to paying duty on what they had brought in, each miner also had to prove he or she was sufficiently supplied for a year. While in the Yukon, miners would also find it necessary to register at regularly established posts between there and Dawson as insurance in case of an accident and as a means of apprehending criminals. In short, this was where miners met up with their first real representatives of law and order, the Royal Northwest Mounted Police.

As it turned out, it was the one touch of sanity which helped to solidify the aims of this ragged army of fortune, many of whom had pawned or sold all they possessed on the elusive chance of striking it rich. Only those who were prepared to lose would be able to tackle the task which lay ahead, that of survival itself. And even then, the

---

On top we prowled through gloomy ruins which time and weather had twisted until little was left to identify them, except to say that they might once have offered some degree of shelter, cribbing for the tramway, or customs buildings—for we were now on the Canadian side.

Opposite: At the international boundary on the summit, Royal Northwest Mounted Police checked each stampeder to be sure he had a year's worth of supplies.

CANADIAN CUSTOM HOUSE ... COPYRIGHT 98. E.A. Hegg.

odds were stacked on the debit side. As a result, many Klondikers owed their lives to the efficiency of the Mounties and the rigid restrictions they imposed.

For the Klondikers, descending was almost as difficult as the climb had been. Rough-locked sleds skidded down a slope corrugated by blizzards and polished by traffic into belts of glossy ice. From here on the trail was mostly downhill, though not without hazard. Transportation varied according to the time of year. The majority of the stampeders climbed the Chilkoot in winter and, once across the pass, could avail themselves of the ice-covered lakes which form a chain leading to lakes Linderman and Bennett. Summertime travelers used boats and canoes that had to be packed over the Chilkoot along with the rest of their gear. Still ahead were long months in the sawpits and the task of building a boat that would carry them down the Yukon.

We were now in an area of the chain of lakes leading to Lake Linderman and Lake Bennett, a region of rugged beauty in the summer.

The shelter was minimal at best. With no dry wood available, we faced the prospect of a wet night without a warm fire. So, urged on by the menacing sky, we headed toward Linderman ten miles away.

Opposite: *Looking down Crater Lake from Chilkoot summit.*

Klondike accommodations were rustic to say the least. (Considering how they got there, it's remarkable that there were any accommodations at all.) Quoting from Fanny Ostrander's diary:

We are staying at the Hotel Linderman. It is funny to call it a hotel, the only thing right up is the price, $7.00 per person per day. It is a log house very poorly built. The first room one enters is the office, bar and dining room all in one with a big air-tight stove in the middle and a shelf with towel, soap and water in one corner. Here we are all supposed to make our toilets, men and women. We have seen the last of white dishes on the table. Everything is granite and tin. Upstairs in the "swell" hotel are the sleeping apartments. Bunks, put up around the room with canvas instead of mattresses, two pair of blankets and a pillow of cotton batting. Two of the bunks are screened from inquisitive eyes for the ladies. This is my retreat when I don't sit in the barroom with the fellows. The entire furniture for this room consists of two bunks, a soap box with a bottle on it and a candle stuck in the bottle. There's also a bucket for what use I've no idea unless it's for toilet papers. John and I made quite a pleasant acquaintance today, a gentleman from Missouri, and we were invited tonight for dinner.

It was hard to believe that Crater Lake had once boasted a restaurant of sorts. Not that we wanted to trade places with the earlier customers, but we had to admit that in this instance, they had the edge on us.

Opposite: *Crater Lake featured a restaurant, the first the stampeders had seen since Sheep Camp.*

INTERIOR OF RESTAURANT AT CRATER LAKE.

SEPT. 4, 1898.

71

In April of '98, while thousands holed up at Sheep Camp and The Scales, waiting to take their turn at old Chilkoot, those who had made it to the other side found things a little more to their liking. In addition to the aerial tramway provided by the Chilkoot Railway and Transportation Company ("railway" was a grandiose title not to be confused with an actual railroad, since it wasn't), there were horses to help them along. The horses, with the exception of the few that had climbed over the Peterson trail on the Chilkoot, had come up by way of the White Pass.

The canoes which had been laboriously packed over the trail became a satisfactory means of transportation. The lakes linked to Bennett were available for paddle and portage. Unfortunately, there were those who felt they could also be used on the Yukon River and chanced the swift currents and deadly rapids, probably out of sheer desperation. Stampeders hoping to get transportation on river steamers found fares raised beyond their ability to pay. Or if they could pay, they were doomed to a long wait.

The trail to Bennett was littered with old conveyances, wagons, canoes, and sleds in various stages of dilapidation. Once an army had filed through this valley intent only on the distant goal and the dreams of a city at the headwaters of the Yukon.

Opposite: Looking back up to the Chilkoot summit from Crater Lake, showing the aerial tram.

LOOKING UP THE CHILKOOT SUMMIT FROM CRATER LAKE SHOWING THE

Lumber was scarce. Therefore, many of the sleds contained boat-building supplies and construction framework, as most would have to build their own boats rather than rely on steamers. For Bennett and Linderman, their location at the headwaters of the Yukon offered some degree of permanency in the years to come.

After Crater Lake comes Long Lake, then Deep Lake, then Linderman. For our crew, it had been a long day. We had risen early to climb the pass and were suffering the minor annoyances brought about by fatigue and distance. Although he was reluctant to admit it, Lyle's feet were blistering badly from a new pair of boots he had purchased just before the trip and had not properly broken in. The rain-soaked packs, heavy to start with, had worn painful grooves into our shoulder muscles. The frequent stops, occasioned by our need to film and reload, only added to the irritation. We all felt it, and tempers flared and subsided like rain squalls on the horizon.

For two years, winter and summer, this had been one of the main thoroughfares leading to the Klondike. Then as suddenly as it began, it ended. I was reminded again of the Bard of the Yukon, Robert Service: "The nameless men who nameless rivers travel and in strange valleys greet strange deaths alone. The intrepid ones who would unravel the mysteries of the polar zone."

Opposite: *Stampeders pulling their sleds on Crater Lake. Some fashioned sails from blankets and canvas to catch winds sweeping down from the pass.*

CRATER LAKE DYEA TRAIL   COPYRIGHT 1898

95.

In short, we had begun to experience something of what the early Klondikers must have felt when burdened beyond belief and fighting the clock. Winter would lock the Yukon under six feet of ice and, caught with dwindling supplies, they would be stopped short of their goal.

Robert Service wrote in "The Ballad of Gum Boot Ben,"

> And so it fell on me a spell of wanderlust was cast.
> The land was still and strange and chill, and cavernous and vast;
> And sad and dead, and dull as lead, the valleys sought the snows;
> And far and wide on every side the ashen peaks arose.

In the snow-covered hills that flanked Lake Linderman, burdened figures moved. Heading back, empty sleds returned for another load. After relaying their supplies and fighting the slippery trail, the stampeders floundered in the soft snow. The experience of the pass had toughened them to accident, and death and wretchedness had made them insensitive to each other. Men died of disease in tent after tent and no one but a partner would take the time to bury them. When one partner died, the other usually gave up and turned back. It didn't look like a country a man could tackle alone.

Our trip over the pass and to the lakes beyond proved as arduous as it had been for the Klondikers.

Opposite: *Crater Lake in September 1898.*

CRATER LAKE, CHILKOOT TRAIL. 464. SEPT. 5, 1898.

For the stampeders, Linderman was where the trail of the land ended and the trail of the water began. In the early months of 1898, they clustered by the thousands around these headwaters of the navigable Yukon. Fanny Ostrander called it "Camp Profanity."

As the men swear from morning to night! Last night I stood outside the tent waiting for John, who was tugging provisions up the hill, and I heard one man say to another, "Look at that woman! I would like to take a snapshot of her and send it home!" Then they all laughed. I know I look like an old witch, but those remarks were not pleasant and I can't bear that man! I rode on his sled yesterday drawn by five dogs. The leader was a particularly lazy dog and all day long the man kept up this cry, "Mush on, Yukon! Mush on!" The dog's name was Yukon. Tomorrow we go further down the lake and hope to establish our camp there til we go down the river. To say that I enjoy camp life here would be a lie, for I don't. It's awful dirty and messy but I hope things will be better in our next camp.

I'll never forget coming upon the collapsed remains of a wagon which looked for all the world as though it had simply grown tired of standing there and decided to rest. It sprawled in a heap like the proverbial "One Hoss Shay." Even the shattered sideboards bore vestiges of the original paint. Fortunately, Linderman was not too far away or I would have been tempted to join it!

Opposite: *Unloading freight on the south end of Long Lake, September 1898.*

UNLOADING FREIGHT, SOUTH END OF LONG LAKE, CHILKOOT TRAIL. 466. SEPT. 14, 1898.

79

Between Linderman and Bennett was Linderman Rapids—a brief taste of what was in store when they started down the Yukon. Still to come was the voracious canyon called "Miles," a precipitous gorge where the river caromed between narrow walls and disgorged boats, men, and gear in a wild melee of action. Still to come was wave-crested Whitehorse Rapids, around which they built a five-mile portage and eventually bypassed with a railroad. Such an obstacle was to claim over 150 boats sunk or smashed in the first few weeks following the river's break-up. 🐾

At last, Linderman! And still clear enough to see the snug outlines of the shelter, even at 10:30 p.m.!

We were welcomed by members of the Canadian trail-building crew, whose efforts we had seen along the way and applauded as much as our tired bodies would permit.

LINDEMAN.

Lake Linderman (also spelled Lindeman and Lindman), housed a canvas city of thousands of stampeders.

Opposite: *Treacherous rapids lay in wait beyond Linderman.*

Chapter Six

The Yukon

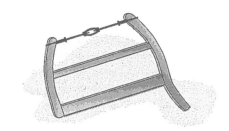

Lake Bennett, the head of navigation on the Yukon, was also the converging point for the White Pass trail which started at Skagway and the Chilkoot which began at Dyea. It became the major staging area for the two streams of Klondikers bent on reaching the gold fields via the Yukon River.

Early in 1898 an estimated 10,000 stampeders were at Bennett, 10,000 more at Lake Linderman, with another 20,000 on their way up from Skagway and Dyea. At Bennett the stampeder could soothe his aching muscles with a hot bath and a shave, hoist a shot of "red-eye," and dine in comfort. He could also buy a boat for upwards of $300 if he had the money. Most of them didn't, so they built their own. Since lumber was scarce and expensive, they obtained boat-building material from the surrounding hills—green timber, mostly whip-sawed by hand.

Wrote Fanny Ostrander:

April 18, 1898: We arrived here about 3:30. Started out yesterday morning hoping to reach Bennett but after a hard day's travel had to make camp about three miles above here. We had an old Dutchman to help us, and he was such a good natured old sort. Helped John pitch the tent and we made him stay for a cup of coffee, as he had to go back 20 miles before reaching his own camp. We're comfortably fixed and I can stand up straight in the tent and don't have to go squatting around. There are a number

Opposite: *Klondikers' camp on Lake Bennett, June 1, 1898.*

KLONDIKERS CAMPING AT LAKE BENNETT JUNE 1ST 1898. COPYRIGHT 1898

of camps here and the sawmill makes so much noise it's like being back in civilization again.

April 19, 1898: We are camped where the Johnson's are camped and today Mrs. Johnson, her children and I took a ride on the lake with the dogs. It was fine sport and I thought of the little folks at home and how they would enjoy it, though I wouldn't have them here for all the gold in the Yukon. This morning, John went down to Caribou Crossing to see if he could find the Johnson's tent [which had hired men which the Ostranders had brought with them from their home in Juneau to help them over the trail] but no sign. We also had a little excitement caused by our tent catching fire from the stove pipe. Burnt quite a hole in it.

April 23, 1898: The men commenced work on the boat today.

April 24, 1898: Dominion Day. I washed my underwear. Small job after wearing it for two weeks. We each took a sponge bath, worth mentioning as it doesn't occur often on your trip to the Yukon.

April 26, 1898: Today is John's birthday. He celebrated by working hard on the boat. The weather is beautiful and seems to be getting warmer all the time.

In the rush to get ready the nearby hills quickly became denuded as Klondikers scrounged for suitable construction material. Enterprising opportunists set up a steam-driven sawmill but couldn't keep up with the demand and it soon became every man for himself. For the average Klondiker, pressed for time and money, an "arm-strong mill," a hold-over from pioneering ancestry, provided the only solution. Men dug a sawpit, then leaned skids against a platform so they could roll logs into place via the skids. They removed the bark and sapwood and marked out the slabs with a chalkline.

Then the work began! They made their cuts with a whipsaw, a long, coarse-toothed instrument which the stampeders declared had

Opposite: *Klondikers whipsawed lumber and built boats that would carry them through a series of lakes and rivers to the gold fields.*

been conceived in hell and wished on them by the Devil himself! One man stood on top; another in the pit. It didn't make any difference which end of the saw you found yourself on, it was a poor choice either way. The man on top bore the weight of the saw, while the man below labored in a shower of sawdust. It took approximately 800 board feet to build a boat capable of carrying a ton of supplies, and the Klondikers won every foot the hard way.

Klondikers claimed that the long hours in the sawpits ruined more good friendships than any institution since marriage. Tempers, already worn thin by the rigors and hardships of the trail, frequently snapped under the strain and erupted in a flurry of fist fights and hard feelings. Some partners even went so far as to cut the completed boat in half in order to satisfy disgruntled demands for an "even split." Many had never hammered a nail or sawed a board or handled a caulking iron, yet slowly but surely an armada took shape and form.

As work progressed, the Mounted Police unit stationed at Bennett and Linderman circulated among the boat builders, warning them to "build them strong and not start out in a floating coffin."

For Fanny Ostrander, life also had its problems:

> **April 28, 1898:** Sent letters home this morning. We got a paper. Seemed good to read of the doings of the outside world. Camp life is a might dull and monotonous. Will be glad to move on. Weather is beautiful. Haven't had a bit of rain since we came and everything indicates an early break up of the ice.
>
> **May 1, 1898:** Today is May Day and really warm enough for a picnic. We took the dogs and went for a ride. They ran away, upsetting the sled and I bumped my head on the ice and for a few minutes I saw stars.

Opposite: *After trimming limbs, workers hoisted the log onto a frame over a pit. One man pulled the saw up and his partner pulled it down in a shower of sawdust.*

May 2, 1898: Still we wait for the ice to thaw and it is tiresome indeed. Our boat is finished, all but the caulking. It is a fine, large boat and I hope we will make the trip safely. Still no news of our men [the hired help] and sometimes I wonder if all is straight. They certainly act very strange. Unless they are sick or met with an accident, we can't find any excuse for them. However, we will not cross our bridge until we reach it. [It was not unusual for a man, employed to help another to get to Dawson, to become afflicted with gold fever himself and desert for what he hoped were greener pastures.] We are both so well and eat and sleep like children. John looks so much better than when we left Juneau. The ice is getting very unsafe. One poor fellow fell through while on his way to LeBarge and was drowned. Am afraid something will happen to Mrs. Frimmick and Mr. Richards who went down yesterday. Their boat was a miserable affair. [Mrs. Frimmick was carrying a load of women's clothes to Dawson. She and Richards met and were married on the trail. They survived the trip.]

May 3, 1989: Nothing happened worth note. Camp here is monotonous to the extreme.

May 6, 1898: Positively nothing to write about today either.

May 8, 1898: Spent the day reading. The wind blew. A little cold. Otherwise the weather is pleasant.

May 9, 1898: The men commenced building the small boat this morning. A "dinky" boat, John calls it. Went out in the woods to gather pitch for the boats. Mr. Cook brought us down some fresh fish for dinner.

May 11, 1898: More pitch was needed so we went out again.

May 12, 1898: Baked bread and sent a loaf up to Mr. Goetz. The men moved down to the beach today already to slide into the water. Another week almost gone for which we are truly thankful. We are all getting impatient to start out, but the ice melts slowly.

May 14, 1898: Same old program. Went up on the mountain to find some flowers but was not successful. John had his tooth out this morning and mussed and fussed all day, ala Mrs. Prissy!

Opposite: *Lake Bennett. M.H. Drake photograph.*

Scene from Lake Bennett during construction

En route to Klondyke Gold Fields

91

May 17, 1898: Still we wait and the ice changes very little.

May 18, 1898: Caulked the seams of the boat today.

May 19, 1898: Launched and christened her the "J and O" this afternoon.

May 20, 1898: We had a little variation this morning. A snowstorm which was really beautiful. Such large flakes, which soon melted.

May 21, 1898: I made a jelly this morning out of dried apples which was fine. It takes an active brain to make sufficient change in our diet for health.

May 22, 1898: Had a headache all day being kept awake by noisy neighbors.

May 23, 1898: Same old routine.

May 24, 1898: Queen's birthday. But hardly anyone in camp is aware of it because we are loyal Americans.

May 29, 1898: I have missed writing because there is so little change in our monotonous camp life. I don't think I was ever so tired of anything in my life as our stay here. The ice is breaking and quite a number have moved on, but the lake is not open and it's useless to move until it is. Mr. Goetz, our German friend, went away Saturday but I don't think he got very far. The mosquitoes have appeared and promise to be an awful trial. John painted the name on our boat Friday, the J & O.

By now, Lake Bennett boasted the largest tent city and greatest boat-building center in the world. By Mounted Police count, a total of 7,124 boats were ready for the trip downriver when the ice broke. It was a fantastic flotilla of skiffs, scows, canoes, barges, and rafts; anything that would float and much that wouldn't. Stationed at the foot of Lake Marsh, the Mounted Police turned back any man who didn't have at least 700 pounds of grub, and a total of 30 million pounds of food floated down to Dawson in the first months of summer.

Where once a horde of axemen demolished the forest, timbered slopes marched to the water's edge. Where once was heard the ring of steel, the whine of saws, and the roaring voice of an army, there was only silence.

Opposite: *Sailing calm water was the easy part of the trek.*

On May 30, 1898 the ice broke. Within a few days, hundreds of homemade craft moved with the gentle wind toward the Klondike. The long months of struggle on the passes and in the sawpits had ended. Ahead lay Dawson, 550 miles away, the golden Mecca at the end of the trail. It was easy to forget that stampeders still faced treacherous Miles Canyon and the turbulence of Whitehorse Rapids.

Our crew reached the railroad tracks which mark the end of Lake Bennett on the morning of our fourth day on the journey. We stopped long enough for Lyle to pose next to a sign which had been recently placed there for the benefit of hikers, most of whom prefer to take the reverse route, since it is easier than hiking up from Dyea. All told, we had covered about thirty miles and there was still a three-mile jaunt to Bennett Station where we could catch the train back to Skagway.

As head of navigation, the settlement at Lake Bennett had swelled in the tide. But even as it grew, it carried within itself the seeds of failure. Marking its end were the ribbons of steel which pointed north toward Whitehorse, linking Skagway to the interior of the Yukon. With the tracks' completion, Bennett became a weigh station important only to the White Pass and Yukon Railway. Today, Bennett continues to serve that purpose and the only surviving remnant of the gold rush in Bennett Station, short of the railroad itself, is an old church vacant and deserted when we visited.

Lyle on the railroad tracks at the end of Lake Bennett.

An old church and the railroad tracks were the only surviving remnants of the gold rush when we reached Bennett.

Opposite: *Bennett in February 1900.*

BENNETT. FEB 13 1900

Epilogue

Why did they do it? There was gold, of course, but historians like to think there was something else. And perhaps they're right. There is in all of us, at times, an urge to see what it is like beyond the next mountain, and the Klondike provided a tempting prospect. The Klondike in many ways simply gave an excuse to break loose from the dismal depression which stifled the 1890s. From that standpoint, borrowing from the innate curiosity and mobility which marked our beginnings in America, it was a natural phenomenon. We had always found the answer by moving west, and when we ran out of "west," there was still the north.

But I like to think it was more than that. The gamble itself! And the step-child born of myth and reality known as luck, plus that solitary seeking which will never know the end because there is none.

In the words of Robert Service who, perhaps, knew the Klondikers better than they knew themselves:

Let us probe the silent places,

let us see what luck betides.

Let us journey to a lonely land I know.

There's a whisper in the night wind,

there's a star a-gleam to guide us,

and the wild is calling...calling...let us go.

Appendix A

The Trail Today

by Carolyn Street LaFond

When Don McCune and the *Exploration Northwest* crew made their trek across the Chilkoot Pass in 1969, the trail had only recently been opened to summer hikers. Not since the gold rush days have many hikers attempted to brave the trail during the winter months. The literature that both the Canadian and American national parks services make available warn of "severe and unpredictable weather, extreme avalanche hazards, and absence of park personnel and doubtful firewood supplies" during the winter. Hikers are advised not to undertake the trail between October and May unless they have "extensive winter travel skills." Although off-season permits are available, a winter journey is strongly discouraged.

However, between May and September, both the Chilkoot and White Pass are popular hiking routes and the trail is considered "rugged" but by no means "a wilderness trail." The busiest period is from mid-July to mid-August when up to eighty hikers daily take to the now well-marked trail. In the summer, Skagway plays host to those wishing to recapture what historians have called, "The Last Great Adventure." With its gold rush buildings and walking tours, Skagway has become the centerpiece of the Klondike Gold Rush National Historic Park.

Most well-supplied hikers, carrying no more than thirty to fifty pounds, can make the trail in four to five days. Determined hikers carrying less can do it in three. The trail has recently become popular for ultra-marathoners who, with only water in hand, do the trail from

Dyea to Bennett in about nine and a half hours! Athletic shoes are known to wear out in this singular "jog" across the pass.

Most hikers begin their trek at the visitors' center in Skagway where a Chilkoot trail orientation video can be seen. Registration and permits for overnight camping on the trail are available at the Dyea ranger station, now considered the "gateway" to the trail. Since hiking the pass involves crossing the U.S. border into Canada, hikers must clear U.S. customs in Skagway at the White Pass Railroad depot. The railroad, called the "Scenic Railway of the World," offers special trail service for summer hikers who have finished the Chilkoot trail and wish to travel from Bennett back to Skagway.

The trail conditions out of Dyea are quite steep and this is often where hikers give up. However, from Finnigans Point to Canyon City the trail is flatter, due to the lowlands in this area, and is easily identified by both orange markers and pyramid rock piles. The trail becomes rough from Canyon City to Sheep Camp, which is the stopping point for most hikers before they head over the pass. The original stampeders' Sheep Camp can't be reached since that part of the trail has washed out over time, but the current shelter for hikers is well-supplied for overnight camping.

Following Sheep Camp, even the most veteran hiker will find the boulder fields "wearing." Here the winds out of the pass are also very strong. The summit of the pass is half a mile from The Scales and this most trying segment of the trail can take anywhere from one-and-a-half to two-and-a-half hours, depending on the amount of weight carried. After the summit, Happy Camp is the first shelter on the Canadian side. It is occasionally bothered by the presence of grizzly bears. However, the trail is well-patrolled by American park rangers and Royal Canadian Mounted Police. In an emergency, there are areas where anyone suffering from hypothermia or injury can be airlifted from the trail. An interpretive trail awaits at Linderman City on the last leg of the journey before Bennett.

Today, the motive for undertaking the Chilkoot Pass is to see a little bit of history but not to make history. Along the way, those artifacts left by the stampeders make nostalgic markers for the trail and link current hikers with the original hikers in their quest for gold. Of course, today, the only gold is in the memory and significance of what came before.

Jessica Lawrence of Olympia, Washington, a descendant of Klondikers, climbed the Chilkoot Pass the summer of 1995 at the age of fifteen. In speaking of the experience, she gratefully acknowledged the advantages that current hikers have with modern-day boots and gear. Upon seeing the last weathered tombstone of an unknown Klondiker, which stood in the boulder fields before the steepest part of the climb, she could only stop to think, "Was it worth it?"

Carolyn Street LaFond is a writer whose work has appeared in various Northwest publications. She is a graduate of the University of Washington where she was much influenced by the late poet and teacher, Nelson Bentley. She currently writes fiction and has completed a historical novel based on the life and times of Renaissance painter Sandro Botticelli. Carolyn lives with her family in Olympia, Washington.

Appendix B

Don McCune

by Linda McCune

Don McCune, the first of five children of Ed and Grace McCune, was born on December 29, 1918 in Thief River Falls, Minnesota. The family moved to Illinois, where two brothers and two sisters were born.

Don graduated from West Aurora High School in Aurora, Illinois, in 1937. Following graduation he left home with three dollars in his pocket and hitchhiked to Washington state to work on his grandfather's farm near Grand Coulee Dam, then under construction. He stayed a year and then joined the Civilian Conservation Corps. Don became a surveyor and lived at the Icicle River Camp in Cashmere, Washington.

He married and soon had two children, Alan and Julie. During World War II, Don moved his family to Seattle and worked at Todd Shipyard. He also tried to enlist in the army twice, but was classified as 4F both times because of flat feet.

While working in the shipyard, he also enrolled in the University of Washington, taking one class in radio broadcasting. His professor, Ted Bell, also the manager of KRSC Radio in Seattle, recognized Don's speaking talent and rich baritone voice.

Don quit college and became a disc jockey on KRSC in 1943. There he worked with the famed Leo Lassen, broadcasting baseball from Sick's Stadium in Seattle. Don also did live, big-band broadcasts from the Trianon Ballroom. He secretly made a 78 RPM recording of his singing "The Story of Sorrento," which he played on his radio shift, never mentioning the artist. It became the song listeners most requested. Soon his radio job developed into a full-time career.

He moved on to KING Radio where he worked until he began to have voice problems, due mostly to long hours and overuse. That year he and his wife divorced, and in 1949 he accepted a job in Fairbanks, Alaska, as station manager for KFAR Radio. He eventually went back on the air, creating the popular radio program, *From Out of the North*, a series of tales of the north country.

He remarried and adopted his wife's son, Gary, and together they had a son, Craig. Later he divorced again.

With the invention of television, Don put KFAR TV on the air in 1952 as station manager and served as an NBC correspondent from Alaska. He was a television pioneer at a time when no one had any idea what to do with this new medium of communication.

In 1957, KOMO TV in Seattle held auditions for a new children's program called *The Captain Puget Show*. Don won the role and moved back to Seattle. In 1958 he won the National Sylvania Award for the best locally produced children's show in the nation. Captain Puget sang sea chanteys and songs about the Pacific Northwest, and took kids on short filmed adventures around the region. A young girl moved to Seattle in 1962, and upon seeing the captain on television, declared that she would grow up and marry him. She did. *The Captain Puget Show* ran for nine years, until 1966.

It was a natural progression while doing *The Captain Puget Show* for Don to evolve into the series *Exploration Northwest*, which began in 1960, also on KOMO TV. These were half-hour adventures filmed in Alaska, Yukon Territory, British Columbia, Washington, Oregon, Idaho, and Montana. Don went on all the film excursions, wrote the scripts, and narrated the shows, which won twenty-six Emmy Awards for excellence in production. Interestingly enough, although he was Don McCune doing *Exploration Northwest*, the people in the Northwest called him Captain Puget—who just happened to now be doing *Explo-*

ration Northwest. He would be fondly called Captain Puget by fans the rest of his life.

He continually returned to Alaska to film a variety of episodes for *Exploration Northwest*. The Yukon gold rush fascinated Don, because, like the gold rushers, he too had gone to Alaska to seek his fortune. Don and the film crew retraced the trail to the Klondike in 1969 and 1970, making five separate episodes which told the entire epoch event. Don felt that these shows were among his best lifetime efforts. Because of this, in 1971, he wrote a manuscript from his TV scripts about the crew's climb of Chilkoot Pass, thinking perhaps he could get it published for the seventy-fifth anniversary of the gold rush. Unsuccessful in that publication effort, he tucked the manuscript away in his desk drawer where it remained until his death.

KOMO TV also assigned Don to host another series from 1962 to 1977 called *Challenge*, an inter-faith dialogue between a rabbi, priest, and minister who took turns leading the discussions on pertinent moral issues of the day. It was Don's job to write an introduction for the discussion and introduce it on camera before turning it over to the panel. Through these three roles in television, *Captain Puget*, *Exploration Northwest*, and *Challenge*, Don helped shape and define the very character of television in the Northwest.

In 1970, Don McCune married his biggest fan, Linda Street, the young girl who first knew him as Captain Puget and had been writing fan letters since she arrived in Seattle in 1962. Don and Linda were married on Rialto Beach near LaPush, Washington, a spot where Don had proposed to her. Together they had three children, Zane, Clint, and Grace.

In 1981, Don authored the book *Washington*, photographed and published by Duane D. Davis. That year, KOMO TV took *Exploration Northwest* off the air. It had run for twenty-one years, longer than any network show. Don decided to retire from KOMO TV that year. He continued to write and narrate video productions on a freelance basis, but mostly he wanted to be actively involved with his three children, who were now in grade school.

He stayed involved with many environmental and service groups. He was most active within the National Academy of Television Arts and Sciences, where he had been the founding father, serving as local president, national vice president, and national trustee. NATAS presented him with both The Governor's Award and the Silver Circle Award.

He was also involved in his community of Woodinville, Washington, in the role of scoutmaster of Boy Scout Troop 422, Hollywood Hill Saddle Club president, and liturgist and council member at his church. He took time to volunteer in his children's classrooms, reading stories, going on field trips, and bringing copies of his *Exploration Northwest* episodes to Washington state history classes.

In 1992, with the Maritime Bicentennial Celebration of the discovery of Northwest waters in full swing, Don and Linda produced, along with composer/arranger Craig Jensen, a recording of Captain Puget songs titled *Looking Back with Captain Puget*. This led to many requests for personal appearances of Captain Puget and he dug out his old captain's hat and complied. With the album a big hit in the Northwest, Don and Linda—again with Craig Jensen—produced a holiday album, *Christmas Tides*.

On his seventy-fourth birthday Don was diagnosed with cancer of the pancreas, and after a brief battle, died on March 27, 1993. KOMO TV viewers flooded the station switchboard with calls upon hearing of his death. KOMO responded by producing a half-hour special on his life. They titled it "Looking Back," the same title of his Captain Puget album.

Don rests in the pioneer cemetery in Woodinville, Washington, near where he and Linda made their home. Don's gravestone reads, "Smooth Sailing...and Bye For Now," his familiar slogan from *The Captain Puget Show*. Following his death, Washington State University Press undertook the publication of this manuscript, which Don had originally penned in 1971 and then tucked away in his desk drawer.

Appendix C

"Views of the Klondike Route"

The Legacy of Photographer Eric Hegg

by Gary Christenson

Eric A. Hegg. Courtesy University of Washington Libraries, Hegg. #3091

Why do adventurers risk their lives in their quest to answer the call of far-off places? Why do men and women undertake the hardship and travail of a difficult journey to the far north? During the 1890s, the heyday of the Klondike gold rush, adventuring was a difficult and serious business. Marine navigation to points north was dangerous, and vast tracts of land were marked "unknown territory" on maps. To fleece stampeders of their money, city fathers and company men portrayed the trip to the north country with rose-colored visions of nuggets littering the shores of gravelly creeks over yonder hills. Brochures and newspaper accounts described the Klondike region in glowing terms that were nothing like the geography and climate. They described the journey inland as something akin to an invigorating walk.

Journeying to the gold fields in the late 1890s was an adventure into the unknown. Just getting to the region—to say nothing of extracting the gold from the earth and bringing it back home—was a major logistical and physical undertaking.

Photographer Eric Hegg heard the call of the Klondike gold rush and made the arduous journey north in the fall of 1897. Why did he go?

Many have tried to explain why people search for gold. Robert Service said it best in the last stanza of his famous poem, "The Spell of the Yukon":

There's gold, and it's haunting and haunting;
It's luring me on as of old;
Yet it isn't the gold that I'm wanting
So much as just finding the gold.

Finding the gold was the important thing. Succeeding at what one set out to do mattered the most in the end. For as history attests, the yellow metal soon became meaningless in the gold fields; there was so much of it around that it lost much of its value to many stampeders. When starvation threatened thousands of people in the boom town of Dawson during the winter of 1897-98, no amount of gold could buy food and supplies that were not available. The life of the stampeders was so trying, and the circumstances so difficult, that they'd pay exorbitant prices for otherwise and elsewhere ordinary things. If you're leading a dog's life and you like bacon and eggs, you'll pay a lot to get them if you haven't had them for months. Many of the stampeders quickly spent their gold fortunes on the pleasures life had to offer.

Eric Hegg's entire life was one of adventure, wherever it took him. For him, too, accomplishing what he set out to do mattered, for Hegg did not venture north for gold. He lived for new adventures, following them like a butterfly seeking a mate on the breeze. When the Klondike gold rush began to play out and a new gold strike occurred soon after in Nome, he left Dawson without hesitation to witness and document the new strike. Alaska and the Yukon became part of Hegg's very being.

It is not well known, but Eric Hegg photographed much more than the stampede to the Klondike. On the way to the gold fields he visited Ketchikan, Juneau, Sitka, Wrangell, and Petersburg. In due course, he also visited other towns, such as Valdez, Cordova, and Anchorage.

Like Hegg, I've sauntered the streets and byways of many northern towns. I learned to study and appreciate a place, its people, and its way of life. I too, photographed the scenery, wildlife, and people. But Eric Hegg did it when those towns were mere youngsters, and when taking a picture was much more difficult!

Still, I can identify with Hegg, for nothing in life prepares you for the unique madness of a boom town. I witnessed the oil town rush at Valdez in the late 1970s, bursting with temporary inhabitants drawn by the lure of easy money. Being there is crucial to relating to someone like Hegg. It helps one to understand what a place feels like, what is important, what isn't, and it gives a perspective about the whole affair. It is impossible in words to fully describe the experience to someone else. Nothing matches being there.

True, we have a rich written historical legacy about the Klondike gold rush. There are numerous books and articles about the period, and they are crucial to understanding what happened in the 1890s. But imagine what it would be like to have just the words. How could we begin to understand what happened without photographs? These help to impart that sense of what a place looked like. It's like watching television with the sound turned on, but without a picture on the screen.

If it were not for that era's photographers—men such as the wandering brothers Eric and Peter Hegg, Larss and Duclos of Dawson, Webster and Stevens, Asahel Curtis of Seattle, and Dobbs and Newell of Nome, we would have few photos to show us what happened, what it was like to be there. Hegg was there, and he took hundreds of photos—thoughtful, revealing, now-precious photos about every aspect of life as it was.

Eric Hegg's early years as a photographer trained him to be a keen observer of the evolutionary process of commercial development. His photographs of the fishing, mining, and logging industries in the Bellingham, Washington, area document in wonderful detail how those industries changed the countryside and its people over the years.

Hegg's party enroute to Lake Bennett. The sleds are drawn by goats. A banner lashed to the side of the load on the rear sled advertises his photo business. Courtesy University of Washington Libraries, Hegg #214.

Thanks to Hegg, we have inherited many photos of men trying to succeed at their calling under the most difficult of circumstances.

Hegg's efforts to take photographs were nothing short of super-human. He photographed what he saw as he traveled north to Dyea, Alaska, jumping-off point for thousands of stampeders headed for the trail to the Klondike. In the winter of 1897-98, Hegg traveled from Skagway over White Pass to Lake Bennett. A stunning photo among the snow-studded mountains shows his portable darkroom lashed to one of two sleds drawn by a half-dozen tame goats imported from Oregon. A sign attached to the rear sled reads, "Have you seen these

Hegg's party rests on its way down the Yukon River to Dawson. The closest boat has a small photo darkroom in the cabin, forward. Courtesy University of Washington Libraries, Hegg #338.

views of Alaska; photographs sent to all parts of the world; E.A. Hegg." It was an enormous effort for Hegg to be able to make these photos. He had to heat his developer to prevent it from freezing, and to filter water through charcoal. If he ran out of a chemical, he had to substitute as best he could. The nearest photo supply store was hundreds of miles away!

Worth noting are the contributions of Eric's brother Peter Hegg, who later followed him north to Skagway. Peter preceded Eric over Chilkoot Pass and, with the help of P.B. Anderson, built two boats for the trip to Dawson in June 1898. One of the boats had a tiny cabin and darkroom. Hegg took every opportunity he could to promote his business. On the side of the cabin he painted the words, "Views Of The Klondike Route."

An intriguing photograph shows the two boats tied up to the shore of the Yukon River, three men busily cooking, mosquito netting covering their heads. This is the party of Peter Hegg, P.B. Anderson, Mr. Grant, and most likely Eric Hegg shooting the photo.

Hegg's photographs are not snapshots. Any photographer looking at them knows instantly that here was an artist at work. Hegg had a keen sense for what ought to be included in the record, a fine eye for composition, and an obvious mastery of the technical details of exposure and developing—especially given the extraordinary conditions in which these remarkable photos were made.

Thanks to Hegg we know without question what the muddy streets of Skagway looked like. We can see the dastardly Soapy Smith holding court in the Skagway saloon in the town he owned, ruling everything in his domain with guile, deceit, and thuggery. We have the lesser-known (and more valuable in some ways) historical images of little villages and resting areas along the trails; photos of the almost-unknown aerial tramways that carried, for a price, the outfits of stampeders up to the summit of Chilkoot Pass. We can clearly read the sign on a business housed in a log cabin at Sheep Camp: "Mascot Restaurant—Hot Drinks And Meals."

Hegg took fabulous, revealing photos at Sheep Camp, at the foot of the 1,200 steps in the snow, the last agonizing push to the 3,500-foot summit. These photos clearly show—in ways words never can—the grandeur, scope, and scale of this monumental human endeavor. Scattered everywhere about are men and the detritus of their activity.

A little further up, at the foot of the final ascent to the summit, at a place called "The Scales," packers weighed the supplies they would carry to the summit for a dollar a pound. From here the route was so steep that sled dogs had to be carried over the pass on the backs of packers or stampeders.

Because Hegg was there, we can almost hear the men groaning eerily from these photos of a hundred years ago, as they carry their loads of up to 100 pounds on their backs in the worst conditions imaginable. They had to make up to forty such trips to get their year's worth of food and supplies (required by the Royal Canadian Mounted Police) over the pass. We have Hegg's now-famous photo of the unbroken line of stampeders climbing heel-to-toe up the icy steps of the 35-degree incline to the snow-bound summit of Chilkoot Pass. Because of Hegg, we instantly understand the agony of that climb.

Hegg also photographed the "grease trail," a large groove worn into the snow when stampeders slid on their butts downhill from the summit of Chilkoot Pass to get another pack load of supplies. And Hegg captured the scene of the fearsome April 3, 1898 aftermath of a deadly avalanche that roared down from the summit above Sheep Camp.

Hegg's photos show us the empty vastness of the interior mountains. We have before us sleds "sailing" on the ice of Crater Lake and Lake Bennett, and strange-looking, home-built vessels with square sails plying the waters of Lake Linderman just after the ice broke up in the spring.

We have photos of stampeders running the rapids of the Yukon River in their overloaded, crude crafts and shots of horse-drawn wagons running on tree-trunk tracks, portaging supplies and equipment around the rapids at Miles Canyon and White Horse Rapids. We have shots of earnest little sternwheelers struggling up the Yukon River to bring food, supplies, and the trappings of society to the wilderness.

We can see the instant tent town of Dawson. We know what the interiors of the saloons looked like, how dignitaries and stampeders alike ate dinner, what it was like digging for gold in the bowels of the Klondike.

There are photos of desperadoes and good guys; gamblers and confidence-men; Mounties and exhausted stampeders; whores and laundry women; the rich, the newly rich, and the destitute; the unknown and the famous. A frozen slice of time shows us the booty of a single gold shipment—valued at $1.5 million—leaving Dawson on September 14, 1898.

And we know about the mosquitoes! We see the stampeders trying to protect themselves from the endless hordes of bloodthirsty bugs. It is an old joke that if you are anywhere in Alaska and you want to go to town, all you have to do is spread your arms. Alaska's unofficial "state bird" will take most of you there.

Hegg's photos are the pictorial record of yesteryear. If ever the phrase "a picture is worth a thousand words" applied to something, this moment in history is it. Unfortunately, many of his images were lost because transporting hundreds of heavy glass-plate negatives from place to place proved a major logistical problem. Hegg moved a number of times, from one far-flung place to another.

Some of his glass-plate negatives nearly ended up being incorporated into greenhouses; the priceless images would have been stripped from the glass. Many of his now-precious photos were snatched from an obscure fate only by the most fortunate of circumstances, when people such as Ethel Anderson Becker, who understood the immense historical value of the pictures, acquired and saved them for posterity.

Recently, I contemplated retracing the trail over the Chilkoot Pass during the early summer. As I investigated the logistics and physical demands of such a trip, I soon realized what a daunting adventure it was even today, even though I would travel in summer and take modern equipment and supplies, lightweight clothing, camping equipment, and dehydrated food; even though I'd enjoy some wayside cabins; even though I'd have modern, compact, lightweight camera technology; even though I could wait to have my photographs developed by a commercial photo laboratory.

Hegg had none of these advantages. He had to take **everything** needed to produce photographs on the spot-a bulky view camera, glass plates, printing paper, chemicals, trays, a portable darkroom, plus his camping equipment and a year's supply of food, just like the stampeders. He had to get many hundreds of pounds of supplies and equipment over the pass. In bulky clothing he had to negotiate a primitive, snow-covered trail in bitter cold. In a case of immense understatement, Hegg is quoted as saying in his later years, "Taking pictures of Alaska was the hardest kind of work."

Out of the tens of thousands of stampeders who made it to Dawson, few came away with a significant amount of gold. Most ended up destitute, disheartened, and disillusioned. Many died. But Hegg found the "gold" he sought; a kind of gold vastly more important than the yellow mineral. Hegg found **his** gold when he photographed a grand human enterprise. It was what he set out to do. In the process, Hegg left us a wonderfully rich visual record; a view into times gone by; a keen insight into what the Klondike gold rush was all about. The legacy of Eric Hegg's "gold strike" is his "Views of the Klondike Route"—the rich visual record he left behind.

Gary Christenson is a freelance writer and photographer and a widely recognized steelhead fishing expert. His photographs have appeared in numerous publications, such as *Rod and Reel, British Columbia Sport Fishing, Alaska Magazine,* and *Super Outdoors,* and his articles have appeared in many magazines, including *Fishing Holes, Cycle Guide, Boater's Paradise,* and *Outdoors Unlimited.* Christenson has served two terms as a Washington director of the Northwest Outdoor Writers Association. In 1994, he received the Enos Bradner Award, the Association's highest honor.

Suggested Reading

There are several books about Hegg and the Klondike gold rush. Here are a few that are particularly recommended.

One Man's Gold Rush: A Klondike Album, by Murray Morgan. (Seattle, University of Washington Press, 1967.) Contains 160 of Hegg's photos (many of which are available from the Special Collections department of the University of Washington Library) and a substantial amount of information about Hegg's life.

Klondike '98—Hegg's Album of the 1898 Alaska Gold Rush, by Ethel Anderson Becker. (Portland: Binfords and Mort, 1949; 1958.) Contains many photos by E.A. Hegg. Becker, also known as "Mrs. Klondike," was a sourdough Klondiker of 1898. She knew Hegg as a lifelong friend, and he gave her much of the data about his photos.

Klondike: The Life and Death of the Last Great Gold Rush, by Pierre Berton. (Pierre Berton, 1958.) This is a wonderful book about every aspect of the Klondike gold rush; it is meticulously researched, well-written, and spellbinding.

Souvenir of Alaska and Yukon Territory, by Eric A. Hegg. (Seattle, 1902.)

"The Eric A. Hegg Collection of Photographs in the University of Washington Library: An Index," by Ruth Genevieve Woodruff Ault. (Unpublished master's thesis, University of Washington, 1955.) Includes a bibliography.

—Gary Christenson